Theos – clear thinking on religion and society

Theos is the UK's leading religion and society think tank. With our ideas and content reaching media outlets with a combined circulation of 160 million in the past ten years, we are shaping the hearts and minds of opinion formers about the role of faith in contemporary society by means of high quality research, events and media commentary. We provide a credible, informed and gracious Christian voice in our mainstream public conversations.

The Economist calls us "an organisation that demands attention", and Julian Baggini, the influential atheist philosopher, has said "Theos provides rare proof that theology can be interesting and relevant even – perhaps especially – for those who do not believe."

To learn more, check us out on social media:

twitter.com/theosthinktank | facebook.com/theosthinktank | www.theosthinktank.co.uk

Why we exist

Religion has emerged as one of the key public issues of the 21st century, both nationally and globally. Our increasingly religiously-diverse society demands that we grapple with religion as a significant force in public life. Unfortunately, much of the debate about the role and place of religion has been unnecessarily emotive and ill-informed. We exist to change that.

We reject the notion of any possible 'neutral' perspective on these issues. We also reject the idea that religion is a purely private matter or that it is possible to divide public and private values for anyone.

We seek, rather, to recognise and analyse the ethical ideas and commitments that underlie public life and to engage in open and honest public debate, bringing the tradition of Christian social and political thought to bear on current issues. We believe that the mainstream Christian tradition has much to offer for a flourishing society.

What we do

Theos conducts research, publishes reports, and holds debates, seminars and lectures on the intersection of religion, politics and society in the contemporary world. We also provide regular comment for print and broadcast media and briefing and analysis to parliamentarians and policy makers. To date, Theos has produced over 50 research reports focusing on the big issues impacting British society, including welfare (*The Future of Welfare: A Theos Collection*), law (*"Speaking Up" – Defending and Delivering Access to Justice Today*), economics (*Just Money: How Catholic Social Teaching can Redeem Capitalism*), multiculturalism (*Making Multiculturalism Work*) and voting reform (*Counting on Reform*), as well as on a range of other religious, legal, political and social issues.

In addition to our independently-driven work, Theos provides research, analysis and advice to individuals and organisations across the private, public and not-for-profit sectors. Our staff and consultants have strong public affairs experience, an excellent research track record and a high level of theological literacy. We are practised in research, analysis, debate, and media relations.

Where we sit

We are committed to the traditional creeds of the Christian faith and draw on social and political thought from a wide range of theological traditions. We also work wit[   ]ls and organisations.

Theos was launched with the support of the Archbisho[   ]
Westminster, but it is independent of any particular der[   ]isation,
committed to the belief that religion in general and Ch[   ]mmon
good of society as a whole. We are not aligned with any[   ]hat
Christian social and political thought cuts across these d................

D1437512

Join the discussion by becoming a Friend of Theos

Impact how society views Christianity and shape the cultural debate

The Friends' Programme is designed specifically for people who wish to enter the heart of the current debate. When you join, our commitment is to keep you informed, equipped, encouraged and inspired so that you can be a voice in the public square with us.

As a member of the Friends' Programme, you are provided with:

- *Hard copies of all our latest reports* on the most pressing issues – social justice, welfare, politics, spirituality, education, money, atheism, humanism…
- *Free access to our events.* Theos hosts a number of high calibre speakers (e.g. Rowan Williams, Larry Siedentop, Grace Davie) and debates ('Magna Carta and the future of liberty', 'Does humanism need Christianity?'). As a friend, you will receive invitations to all these without charge.
- *A network of like-minded people* who wish to share ideas and collaborate with one another. We host networking events which help you meet fellow Friends and build your own network, allowing ideas to flow and connections to form.
- *Our monthly e-newsletter* which is your one-stop digest for the latest news regarding religion and society.
- **If you join as an Associate**, you are *invited to private functions with the team*, allowing you to discuss upcoming projects, review the latest issues and trends in society, and have your say in where you see the public debate is going.

You can become a Friend or Associate today by visiting our website
www.theosthinktank.co.uk

If you'd prefer additional information, you can write to us directly:
Friends Programme, Theos, 77 Great Peter Street, London, SW1P 2EZ

If you have any inquiries regarding the Programme, you can email us at:
friends@theosthinktank.co.uk

Christianity and Mental Health: Theology, Activities, Potential

Ben Ryan

Published by Theos in 2017
© Theos

ISBN 978-0-9956543-0-3

Some rights reserved – see copyright licence for details
For further information and subscription details please contact:

Theos
Licence Department
77 Great Peter Street
London
SW1P 2EZ

T 020 7828 7777
E hello@theosthinktank.co.uk
www.theosthinktank.co.uk

contents

acknowledgements

I would like to thank the many people who gave up time and effort to help produce this report. This includes, first and foremost, those who were kind enough to be interviewed about their experiences in the mental health sector and all of those who volunteered information to Theos in response to the call for evidence. Not every lead has been followed up, but I hope that, if and when, we return to this field, we will be able to pursue far more of the ideas and suggestions put forward.

The impetus for this scoping study came from Ian and Sue Aldred, and I am very grateful for their long support of Theos in general, and of this project specifically.

Friends and colleagues at Theos, and my friend Dr David Bishop, have generously helped with the research and have been through various drafts, hopefully eliminating the more egregious errors on my part. Any that have slipped through are of course entirely the responsibility of the author.

Ben Ryan

executive summary

This report follows on from the findings of the Theos report *Religion and Wellbeing: Assessing the Evidence*. That report looked at 140 academic studies and sought to analyse the underlying relationship between religion and wellbeing. This report, by contrast, looks more specifically at Christianity and is **an attempt to assess what Christians are actually contributing to society in terms of addressing mental health needs.**

It should be read as **a scoping study,** an initial foray into the field which is looking to suggest a research agenda, rather than presenting any firm conclusions. It draws on 15 informal interviews with Christian experts and practitioners within the field, representing a range of denominations, theologies, and particular engagements with mental health.

The report provides a brief overview of the mental health situation in the UK today, suggests some Christian principles on which an authentic Christian response could be built, makes a preliminary effort to map such services as already exist, and finally looks to establish how effective those services are and how they could be improved.

Throughout, the report returns to "what next?" questions, outlining a programme of research that is needed to encourage, inform, shape and amplify the Christian response to current mental health problems.

mental health today

The reality of mental health in the UK today is a stark one. Among the more worrying statistics are that:

- Almost ten million British adults are diagnosed with at least one mental health problem each year.[1]

- Around one in four adults in the UK have been diagnosed with at least one mental health problem over their lifetime.[2]

- Mixed anxiety and depression causes an estimated one fifth of all days lost from work in Britain.[3]

- In 2014, 19.7% of people in the UK aged 16 and over showed some symptoms of anxiety or depression, including 22.5% of women.[4]

The recognition of this has caused an increasing level of political attention, with first David Cameron and then Theresa May appointing ministers for mental health and making tackling mental health a government priority. There have also been significant efforts to raise public awareness and to challenge the stigma over mental health, with public figures as diverse as pop stars, sporting heroes and even Princes Harry and William speaking publicly about their experience. Mental health is now a major public issue, raising further the question of what Christians are doing to address these issues and how effective their efforts are proving.

Christian resources for understanding mental health

Developing a distinctive Christian language and approach to mental health has proven difficult. The language of mental health is often highly clinical in nature, and the experience of mental illness is difficult to verbalise and explain to those who do not share it. To that end, this report proposes a set of possible building blocks for developing a Christian approach, drawing from the biblical evidence, from Christian anthropology and from theological reflection. These are set out in chapter 2.

The chapter concludes that we need:

- a careful re-appraisal of how the Bible is used on this topic. Rather than focusing on limited accounts of explicit mental illness, or demonic possession, more attention ought to be paid to the ability to begin **building an authentic Christian language of mental health from the perspective of sufferers**. Where many Christian resources currently focus on raising awareness of different mental health issues, there is more to be done in terms of letting sufferers find a legitimately biblical and theological language to verbalise their own experiences.

- an **analysis of the burgeoning exorcism scene in the UK** in the light of concerns over how it is being used and its possible negative consequences.

- biblical resources that allow for Christians to embrace medical science and **prevent the danger of "over-spiritualising" problems**. There is some evidence of projects in this space already.

mapping Christian initiatives in the mental health field

What counts as a Christian initiative into the realm of mental health is not clear cut. It depends, for example, on where you draw the lines of the definition of mental health. Organisations and individuals who work in the mental health sector can incorporate a range that extends from the primarily medical (some of which are almost 'mechanical' in the sense that they are seeking to fix something that has gone physically wrong), to those whose work is more straightforwardly pastoral (perhaps providing a listening ear, or a respite service).

Chapter 3 of the report outlines various Christian initiatives. It looks at 37 different types of mental health issue, describes each issue, and then lists a number of Christian initiatives engaged in that areas.

There is considerable range and variety here but it is important to emphasise that this is only a scoping study and not a systematic survey of the initiatives currently underway. Accordingly, it concludes that we need **a more systematic study**, that would comprehensively map Christian initiatives. This would require a larger and more sustained project using quantitative data and a broader national survey. The findings demonstrated here are, however, indicative of the spread. The grid demonstrates that there are a great many Christian initiatives across a huge range of areas, though they are often highly localised, small scale and under the radar.

Christian work in mental health: how effective is it?

In addition to exploring the range of Christian initiatives, we also looked at their effectiveness:

- The evidence suggests that religious belief aids resilience in responding to traumatic events and leads to faster recovery from mental health problems.

- Effective Christian initiatives can reduce the burden on the NHS or social services, serving a public good.

- Good resources, including videos, reports, and short guides, which helped to explain mental health to people and how they could help, had all received very positive feedback. Keeping these resources up to date, accessible and online was, however, proving a challenge for those (the majority) who lacked significant institutional backing.

- Conferences and events designed to help people understand and respond to mental health issues were also reported as having been successful – though there was a challenge there in having the people available to provide such events. The lack of available funding for many organisations left them reliant on getting expenses paid by those to whom they were speaking, which was having a detrimental effect on their impact. There was also simply a limited pool of people with sufficient expertise to provide training.

- Some of the most effective work was done with young people. Several Christian groups were working in schools and with young people and had developed means of identifying possible mental health problems at an early stage, as well as training other staff to do the same.

- Mental health in the clergy is a major concern, and an increasing number of schemes and strategies were designed with a specifically clerical focus. Funding, unsurprisingly, was repeatedly listed as a major concern.

- Relationships with statutory and secular bodies were sometimes challenging. There was mixed evidence on this – but some had certainly felt marginalised or excluded on account of being faith-based organisations. This had not, however, stopped Christian initiatives from working across a huge range of areas, often in close partnership with local government, secular charities or NHS trusts.

- Others had struggled to make headway due to limitations from within the Church. There was a sense that there was a lack of a strategy or much joined up thinking from many of the denominations, and that communication and networking were consistent problems.

- There was a perception that relationships within healthcare in particular had improved over recent years, with an increased focus on spiritual needs and care. It was felt that more work needed to be done here, as there were significant regional variations in how seriously spirituality was taken.

- Though interviewees recognised the importance of measuring what they did, many found the expectations of secular bodies (and sometimes church bodies) to be too onerous not to truly reflective of the work being done.

future work needed in light of empirical research

Over and above the grid of Christian initiatives provided in chapter 3, we need to map with more clarity the full scope of Christian activity. Knowing the full picture will be essential before strong proposals for the future can be outlined.

Though we have interviewed a number of Christians on their experiences within secular settings, there is clearly another side to the story and future research will be needed to assess how secular and medical bodies engage with Christian initiatives and where they feel relations could be usefully improved.

The challenge of impact and measurement is going to remain important. Future work on designing measurable impact assessment tools for Christian projects would be beneficial to many, particularly smaller projects.

Greater networking and cohesion between Christians would be helpful in preventing overlaps and developing a strategy which could be more effective in some areas than the piecemeal efforts that presently exist.

Greater clarification of the rules regarding acceptable expressions of faith in an NHS context would help staff be more confident in dealing with faith issues.

There is work to do in making the positive case for spirituality, and more specifically religion, in helping with mental health. There is a growing evidence base that religion and spirituality can be beneficial for recovery and wellbeing and that people want their spiritual and religious needs addressed within the medical and care sectors, but there is still a sense in which secular bodies have been wary about embracing such opportunities.

executive summary – references

1   McManus S, Meltzer H, Brugha T, Bebbington P, Jenkins R (eds), 'Adult Psychiatric Morbidity in England 2007: results of a household survey.' *NHS Information Centre for Health and Social Care*. (2009). Available at: http://www.hscic.gov.uk/pubs/psychiatricmorbidity07

2   ibid.

3   Das-Munshi J, Goldberg D, Bebbington PE, Bhugra DK, Brugha TS, Dewey ME et al. 'Public health significance of mixed anxiety and depression: beyond current classification.' *Br J Psychiatry*, (2008); 192(3): pp. 171–177.

4   *Office for National Statistics* (2016).

foreword

The evidence that 'religion' is good for 'mental wellbeing' is now incontrovertible. Last year, Theos published a 'meta-study' of over 140 academic papers, disambiguating the various concepts and then examining the relationships between them. The weight of evidence was clear: religion – belief, but even more so personal and corporate religious practice – is good for people's mental (and physical) wellbeing.

As Ben Ryan discusses at the start of this study, the UK has woken up to the seriousness of its mental health problems. The flat-lining of general public wellbeing has long been recognised. The severity of our mental health problems is only just becoming apparent.

The combination of these two points invites an obvious question: if the country is suffering from mental health problems, and religious belief and practice are good for our mental health, what are Christians doing about it?

The answer is "quite a bit", as Ben outlines in chapter 3, but it is probably also "quite a bit less than it could". This report is intended to help begin to move from the first answer to the second.

Christianity and Mental Health: Theology, Activities, Potential is a scoping study. That means it is short and focused more on identifying the questions than delivering the answers. It is based on biblical and theological research and a number of interviews but it is clear that much more work needs to be done in this area.

The report outlines some of the statistics pertaining to mental health in the UK, the biblical and theological resources for a Christian response, and the range of Christian interventions in the field, and then explores how successful and well-received (or otherwise) they have been. All the way through it points to what more needs to be done to help strengthen the Christian response. It is, in effect, the foundations on which we hope much more detailed and broader research and response can be constructed.

It is our hope that readers will not only be encouraged by the kind of activity that is already underway in churches and Christian charities across the country, but will also catch the vision of a fuller and deeper Christian response – and will get in touch with us at Theos to help us in our pursuit of that goal.

Nick Spencer
Research Director, Theos

introduction

The issue of mental health has been gaining public attention in recent years. Awareness-raising efforts across a number of fields (notably the efforts of Princes William and Harry to open up about their struggles in the wake of their mother's death) have significantly increased public interest and concern. There have been warnings for some time, with dire statistics from various agencies – including from the Health Survey for England report in 2014 which reported that one in four British adults had been diagnosed with a mental health issue during their lifetime.[1]

That, and other reports, has prompted a political response. In his last months in office, David Cameron made significant moves towards a "revolution in mental health", appointing the first minister for mental health (a position kept by his successor Theresa May) and unveiling a new national strategy. May's government has also committed to put mental health as a priority area.

At the same time, there has been a steady growth in interest in the relationship between religion and mental health. This is not a new issue, Freud famously had much to say (little of it positive) about religion and psychology. However, an increasing amount of research has tried to analyse the relationship in depth. Many of these studies were summarised in the Theos report *Religion and Wellbeing: Assessing the Evidence* (2016), which drew on 140 academic studies and concluded that, on the whole, there was a positive correlation between religion and wellbeing, albeit that both terms requires careful clarification. In particular, *Religion and Wellbeing* identified that "the more serious, genuinely held and practically-evidenced a religious commitment is, then the greater the positive impact it is likely to have on wellbeing".[2]

Where that report looked to explore the underlying relationship, this study looks instead at what Christian groups are doing to confront the issue. In particular, *Christianity and Mental Health* seeks to explore the question, "What can (and what should) Christians do in this field?" It does so tentatively as, unusually for a Theos report, it is primarily a scoping study, and doesn't pretend to present any fully worked out 'solutions'. *Christianity and Mental Health* is an effort to map the landscape as it currently exists, and to raise questions for future research.

It is based on desk research and 15 informal interviews with Christian practitioners in the field, exploring their experiences. The interviewees represented a range of Christian denominations, and varied significantly in the particular area of mental health they were confronting, from chaplaincy in mental health trusts, through to local respite services, and from providing resources to direct provision of care. Given the scope of the mental health field, these interviews are not meant to be taken as representative of the whole, but they do represent an indicative range of responses.

The first chapter provides a brief overview of the current situation with regards to mental health in the UK, drawing on recent reports. The second provides some Christian resources (both biblical and more broadly theological) that can help to shape an authentically Christian response to mental health. Chapter 3 provides the beginnings of a mapping exercise to establish what Christians are currently doing in this sector. The concluding chapter draws on evidence from interviews to establish how this work is currently going and what could be done to make it more effective. Each chapter has a concluding set of recommendations for further research work that is needed as a result of those findings.

It is our hope that this report marks the start rather than an end of a programme of work looking at Christianity and mental health issues today. The subject is important, and growing in recognition; it speaks to a number of core Christian concerns pertaining to human wholeness and peace, and there are a growing number of Christian/church-based initiatives across the country. We hope that this and subsequent work will make a contribution towards clarifying, equipping, guiding, and inspiring serious Christian engagement with mental health problems in the UK today.

introduction – references

1   Health Survey England 2014 available online at: http://healthsurvey.hscic.gov.uk/
     media/37739/HSE2014-Ch2-Mental-health-problems.pdf

2   Spencer et al, *Religion and Wellbeing: Assessing the Evidence*, Theos (2016), p. 6.

mental health today

In recent years there has been a significant drive to raise awareness of mental health issues in the UK. This has included a number of major initiatives including the Mental Health Awareness Week and efforts to raise public awareness through asking celebrities and public figures to share their experiences. Despite these efforts, and the resulting greater public consciousness, it is difficult not to be shocked by some of the statistics that have been produced.

Among other more striking statistics are the claims that:

- Almost ten million British adults are diagnosed with at least one mental health problem each year.[1]

- Around one in four adults in the UK have been diagnosed with at least one mental health problem over their lifetime.[2]

- An estimated 3% of adults are currently diagnosed with depression, 6% with generalised anxiety disorder, and nearly 8% with mixed anxiety and depression.[3]

- A little under 11% of UK adults have had suicidal thoughts over their lifetime and just under 7% have made a suicide attempt.[4]

- Between 4% and 10% of people in England will suffer depression over their lifetime.[5]

- Mixed anxiety and depression causes an estimated one fifth of all days lost from work in Britain.[6]

- In 2014 19.7% of people in the UK aged 16 and over showed some symptoms of anxiety or depression, including 22.5% among women.[7]

Beyond these general statistics, there are specific concerns for certain sectors. Among groups considered particularly at risk are the homeless, prisoners, victims of abuse, military veterans and children and adults living in the poorest income bracket. Thus, for example, the prison sector has been much in the news, reinforcing older findings that the suicide rate among prisoners is almost 15 times that of the general population.[8] More than 70% of prisoners are thought to have two or more mental health disorders.[9]

Among older people there is a growing body of evidence on the prevalence of dementia, particularly as people continue to live longer. Whether or not dementia is included as a mental health issue depends on the definition used, but it is certainly included as such by a number of organisations and agencies in the sector, including several Christian groups who were looked at as part of this research. What is not in doubt is the severity of the issue. Worldwide the number of people with dementia was expected to double from 2014 levels by 2030.[10]

Similarly, there is especial concern about the mental health of British children and teenagers. Quite apart from consistently scoring poorly in international league tables for happiness[11] there are worrying trends revealing that eating disorders and stress in children are on the increase.[12] Such particular concerns notwithstanding, there is no group or demographic in the UK that is immune to the possibility of developing mental illness.

To some those statistics may seem too extreme as to be likely, and there are legitimate questions to be asked about what counts as a mental health problem and how they can possibly be accurately recorded. Rates of self-harm, for example, are often thought to be under-recorded, while some critics have criticised a culture of too often diagnosing, among others, depression and ADHD.[13] What is surely not in doubt, however, is that our medical understanding of mental health is constantly increasing, and bringing with it an increased awareness of what mental health is, and how the modern world affects upon it. Mental health is now a major policy and medical issue and one which cannot be ignored.

chapter 1 – references

1   McManus S, Meltzer H, Brugha T, Bebbington P, Jenkins R (eds), 'Adult Psychiatric Morbidity in England 2007: results of a household survey.' *NHS Information Centre for Health and Social Care* (2009) Available at: http://www.hscic.gov.uk/pubs/psychiatricmorbidity07.

2   ibid.

3   McManus S, Bebbington P, Jenkins R, Brugha T. (eds.). *Mental health and wellbeing in England: Adult psychiatric morbidity survey 2014.* (Leeds: NHS digital, 2016).

4   ibid.

5   McManus et al. 'Adult Psychiatric Morbidity'.

6   Das-Munshi J, Goldberg D, Bebbington PE, Bhugra DK, Brugha TS, Dewey ME et al. 'Public health significance of mixed anxiety and depression: beyond current classification.' *Br J Psychiatry*, (2008); 192(3): pp. 171–177.

7   'Measuring national well-being: Life in the UK: 2016', Office for National Statistics (2016).

8   'National Service Framework for Mental Health: five years on', Department of Health (2004). http://www.bipsolutions.com/docstore/pdf/9122.pdf.

9   'Mental Health and Social Exclusion: Social Exclusion Unit Report Summary' Office of the Deputy Prime Minister, 2004.

10   Prince M, Albanese E, Guerchet M, Prina M, *World Alzheimer's Report, Dementia and Risk Reduction - An analysis of protective and modifiable factors*, Alzheimer's Disease International (London, 2014).

11   See, for example, 'The Childhood Report 2015', The Children's Society (2015).

12   Micali N, Hagberg KW, Petersen I, Treasure JL, 'The incidence of eating disorders in the UK in 2000–2009: Findings from the General Practice Research Database', *BMJ Open* (2013).

13   See, for example, Thomas R, Mitchell G, and Batstra L, 'Attention-deficit/hyperactivity disorder: are we helping or harming?' *BMJ* (2013) 347:f6172.

Christian resources for understanding mental health

introduction

Across a number of interviews, and regularly remarked upon in blogs and articles by Christians, one comment that frequently arose was the problem of language. The language of mental health sounds medical. There are few directly applicable biblical passages. The very notion of mental health, as a distinct area, is a relatively recent invention. Even within the medical profession the idea of the mind as an organ, or something which can be treated scientifically, is in its relative infancy. Psychiatry is a fast-changing profession, and wider public discourse is only slowly catching up.

This raises a number of particular challenges for Christians in the field. First, how can Christians experiencing mental health issues find a language to talk about their experiences that makes sense in Christian terms? Second, is there a way for the Church more broadly to conceive of mental health within a theological framework?

This chapter presents some tentative building blocks on which a theoretical and theological answer to those questions might be formulated. It looks first at biblical sources for thinking about mental health and then to broader Christian anthropological and, finally, theological ideas.

the Bible and mental health

Looking specifically at examples of mental health issues in the Bible is a difficult process. The language and terminology of medicine has moved so rapidly over the past few decades that there should not be much expectation of clear cut mental health diagnosis in modern terms in ancient biblical texts.

Though the Bible does occasionally refer to what we might consider to be mental illness, we have to treat those sections with caution. For example, in Daniel 4 Nebuchadnezzar is described as having gone mad, and is driven away from his people and lives like an animal, eating grass. 1 Samuel contains details of the madness of Saul, who has "an evil spirit" come upon him, which causes him to irrationally despise David, and even to attempt to murder him (1 Samuel 18:10), later he falls into a "prophetic frenzy".

Both of these cases are talking about madness – but it is impossible at this distance to define what sort of mental health issue Nebuchadnezzar and Saul were suffering from. Nor do these accounts really help us much in terms of how we ought to approach mental health today. They do, however, illustrate that some sorts of mental illness were at least familiar in Old Testament times.

A further set of contentious examples might be drawn from the demonic possession accounts in the New Testament – which some have taken to be examples of mental illness. In fact, this is by no means clear cut, and the symptoms of those possessed in the New Testament do not necessarily match up well with what we know of mental illness. This is an issue which we will return to in more detail below.

Of greater interest for our purposes are those passages that seem to speak to mental illness in a way that can resonate powerfully with sufferers, since these might give us the building blocks for forming an authentic distinctive language for talking about these issues. For example, Psalm 88 is sometimes taken as a passage that speaks very closely to the experience of depression. The psalmist expresses feelings of being cut off and forgotten by God and then laments:

> You have put me in the lowest pit, in the darkest depths. Your wrath lies heavily on me; you have overwhelmed me with all your waves. You have taken from me my closest friends and have made me repulsive to them. I am confined and cannot escape; my eyes are dim with grief. (Psalm 88:6-9)

And

> From my youth I have suffered and been close to death; I have borne your terrors and am in despair. Your wrath has swept over me; your terrors have destroyed me. All day long they surround me like a flood; they have completely engulfed me. You have taken from me friend and neighbour – darkness is my closest friend. (Psalm 88:15-18).

A number of other Psalms (e.g. 13, 42) also contain passages which speak of the psalmist's despair, hopelessness and feeling of isolation. This may provide a stronger basis for building a biblical answer to the question of mental health than the examples of madness given above, since the feelings expressed more closely mirror the experiences of many suffering with conditions including anxiety, depression and isolation. The task of building a language with which to talk about mental health in Christian terms, an issue identified as critical by several interviewees, may be easier if we start from these personal expressions of suffering and isolation than if we start from from accounts of madness in others.

excursus: demons and exorcisms

Perhaps the most contentious aspect of thinking about Christian attitudes to mental health is the degree to which attention is given to the possibility of demonic possession. Certainly there is a biblical warrant for the dangers of demonic forces, and Jesus' great commission to the disciples includes the explicit command to "cast out demons". However, there is also need for serious caution.

For one thing, there is a danger of what one interviewee (a Christian psychiatrist) referred to as "Christian over-spiritualising", by which he meant a tendency to ascribe anything and everything to spiritual causes when other medical ones may exist. Secondly, it is difficult to have certainty over whether what the Bible describes as demonic possession and current mental health issues have any overlap. Certainly there was a degree of scepticism about this among several interviewees. One, a chaplain who described themselves as a "Bible-believing evangelical" who took biblical accounts seriously said that in all their experience with a mental health trust they had "never seen anything I would say that looked like demonic possession, but I've seen plenty of people who have been told that's what they're experiencing by other Christians". Thirdly, if Christians start treating people with mental health issues as if they are possessed when they are not, they run the risk of doing very serious harm.

Some of the symptoms of those possessed can certainly sound like mental health issues. The man possessed by Legion lived among the tombs, could not be restrained and self-harmed (Mark 5:4-5). In other cases the results seem to be simply physical – including blindness (Matthew 12:22-32) or muteness (Matthew 9:32-42). It seems contestable the extent to which possessions can be easily aligned to mental health issues: there is little full detail and it is difficult to read back modern medical diagnosis into limited textual evidence.

Nevertheless, exorcisms are now a booming industry in the UK, with a number of interviewees noting the astonishing increase in demand – often, as one noted, in defiance of any actual rules or procedures put in place by any church, such as 'The House of Bishops' Guidelines for Good Practice in the Deliverance Ministry 1975 (revised 2012)' produced by the Church of England. Part of this has been driven by immigrant communities and Pentecostal churches which are very open about their exorcism services. There are potential dangers to this: without discounting the possibility of demonic possession, the perspective of several Christians working in the mental health sphere said that, in the vast majority of cases, the person in question was suffering with mental health issues which required psychiatric assistance.

Jesus' command was to heal the sick and to cast out demons. The two are not synonymous. Just as for physical ailments we recommend seeking medical assistance, so it must be for mental illness. This is not to discount the possibility of demonic attacks, but it is to apply caution, in order to ensure that we are best looking after the needs of sufferers. One of the frustrations of medical professionals with Christians comes from accounts and anecdotes of people with medical health issues going off their medication because they've been told that prayer is enough, and relapsing as a result.[1] This is a classic example of well-meaning initiative with the potential for serious harm. It runs the risk of becoming a sort of abuse – which can be understood as psychological harm inflicted upon the victim by members of their own religious group. This is clearly an issue of concern, despite the fact that motivations may be good ones, and it will be important to keep a close eye on over coming years.

work that is needed in the light of the biblical evidence:

- There is a need for a re-appraisal of how we use the Bible on this topic. Rather than focusing on limited accounts of explicit mental illness within the biblical story, or on demonic possession as a growing number of UK Christians appear to be doing, we need to develop an authentic Christian language of mental health from the perspective of sufferers. Where many Christian resources currently focus on raising awareness of different mental health issues there is more to be done in terms of helping sufferers find a biblical language to verbalise their own experiences.

- There is need for an analysis of the burgeoning exorcism scene in the UK in the light of concerns over how it is being used and its possible negative consequences.

- There is space for biblical resources that allow for Christians to embrace medical science and prevent the danger of "over-spiritualising" problems. There is some evidence of projects in this space already (see chapter 3 below).

Christian anthropology and mental health

If the biblical evidence around mental illness is somewhat limited, that does not mean there is nothing Christian to be said on the issue. In particular, there are three areas of

Christian anthropology (understanding of what it is to be human) and theology that can help provide a model for how we deal with mental health. The first is our understanding of the mind/spirit/soul and the second is the Christian understanding of human relationality.

anthropology – mind, spirit, soul

Any Christian approach to mental health must answer a fundamental question about where the mind sits within our theory of human existence. Christianity has a distinctive focus on humans as both body and soul, with both being of critical importance. So in 1 Corinthians 6:19 Paul famously warns his audience not to sin against their body because the body is a "temple of the Holy Spirit". Christians are to glorify God with their bodies.

In the incarnation, God takes on the fullness of human bodily existence, including suffering and death. The resurrection is itself a physical and bodily event, as is made clear to Thomas, who is able to put his fingers where the nails had been in Jesus' hands, and his hand in Jesus' side (John 20:26-27). To this, many more examples could be added, but the point is that there is a significant focus on the physical as well as the spiritual element of human existence.

By contrast there is comparatively little on the place of the mind in human existence, which raises an immediate theological challenge. Do supposedly Christian attitudes to mental health owe more to Freud than to Jesus?

The Bible does in fact talk about the mind, though not perhaps in the same way as we might do today. In the Old Testament, the word heart (*leb, lebab*), refers to the inner self, where decisions are made (e.g. 2 Chronicles 12:14), and where wisdom and understanding are located (1 Kings 3:12; Proverbs 16:23). Elsewhere the terms spirit (*ruah*) or soul (*nepes*) are used of the will or internal thought process (e.g. Daniel 5:20). The latter is significant in the famous passage from Deuteronomy 6:5 to "Love the Lord your God with all your heart and with all your soul and with all your strength" which combines *leb* and *nepes* in a single command.

The New Testament, and Paul in particular, talk more about the mind. The Greek word *nous* is used in a range of contexts, including talking about moral inclination, the means of understanding, and the means of determining action. Its associated noun *anoia* is used for a failure to understand, often resulting in a distance from God. A different term *phroneo* is also used, for example in Romans 8, in which the mind governed by the spirit is opposed to the mind governed by the flesh.

There are several conclusions we can infer from these notes. One is that the mind, despite not being thought of in the pathological terms of today's medicine, is certainly present and important in the biblical worldview. In fact, the mind is seen in a number of places as being critical in aiding or hindering our relationship with God. Hardened hearts, or a lack of understanding, are just two of the charges regularly directed towards those who refused and rejected Jesus in the Gospel narratives. Accordingly, there is a clear need for a Christian anthropology that takes full account not only of body and soul, but also of the mind as a key part of what it means to be human.

An integrated human existence demands a fuller appreciation of the mind. Just as Christians are called to make temples of their bodies so, too, a greater emphasis needs to be placed on the need to care for and cultivate the mind. This is all the more true given that although we can talk of these things as separate in principle, in practice it is impossible to abstract one from the others. Poor physical health can cause mental symptoms, and vice versa. Poor health in either can hinder our ability to fully live out our humanity, and place limitations on our ability to be in right relationship with God.

anthropology – relationality

A second aspect of Christian anthropology worth mentioning briefly in the context of mental health is that of relationality. Human beings are not atomised individuals but instead reach their fullness of being in relationship with God and other human beings. In this, the Trinity provides perhaps the most comprehensive model for Christian understandings of relationships. Just as each person of the Trinity (Father, Son and Holy Spirit) cannot exist without relation to the other two in a single Godhead, so human beings too (made in the image of God) are essentially relational beings.[2] The social consequences of this include the idea of the tenet of Catholic Social Teaching which is the Common Good – only by working with others is the fulfilment of each individual accomplished.[3]

Our ability to be in relationships can be strained by issues of mental health. This can be either because the issue itself creates difficulties – anxiety, for example, can make social interactions strained or even impossible – or because the nature of the issue is difficult to communicate. Those struggling with issues can find it difficult to put their experiences into words (and can find that efforts to do so are inadequate or unhelpful[4]) and those who have never experienced the mental health issue in question have no way of understanding or conceiving the experience of the other person.

Further to that, an issue identified in several of the interviews is that of stigma. Some mental health issues are poorly understood (like schizophrenia) and can provoke fear. Common experiences include people not wanting to bring up the subject of a mental health issue for fear of causing offence, saying the wrong thing or making the situation worse. All of this makes the task of forming relationships a potentially difficult one.

This raises a critical issue for the Church and the way it addresses mental health. If human beings are relational, and called to form relationships in order to be fully human and to develop the Common Good, then there needs to be more thought put to the issue of what that means for people with mental health. Some of the schemes mentioned below are already seeking to address that issue, but further integration will be necessary.

work that is needed in the light of the anthropological material:

- Resources and reflection on the place of a healthy mind in a Christian vision of humanity (including biblical guides to terms such as *nous*), and how to cultivate positive mental health in the light of that. In particular further resources on how biblical themes can be matched with current mental health anthropologies in way which is authentic to both theology and the latest medical science.

- Developing services and initiatives on mental health that emphasise the importance of relationality. Many services knowingly or unknowingly already do that,[5] but emphasising it as a deliberate choice and as a key criteria of future projects would both be true to a Christian ethos and make for an effective service.

theology: responsibility, redemption and reconciliation

The point above was to establish a basis for mental health and the mind as being an essential part of human nature which, therefore, demands a Christian theological response. With that established, a number of particular theological issues arise. The first is the theme of responsibility, the second Christian understandings of redemption as they relate to mental health, and the third is the related idea of reconciliation.

responsibility

The first of these is the challenge posed by particular mental health issues to our idea of responsibility. Christian teaching holds that all human beings are fallen and in need of redemption, and are deemed to be held responsible for their own failings. In Matthew 25:31-46 Jesus provides a vision of the final judgement, with people divided according to their actions, with the righteous enjoying eternal life, and the unrighteous eternal punishment. How do we reconcile that with an increasing body of scientific, medical and indeed legal analysis that suggests that particular mental issues diminish the responsibility of individuals?

Psychosis impairs thoughts and emotions such that the sufferer experiences a loss of connection with their external reality. Can such people be held responsible for what would otherwise be considered sinful behaviour? Depression causes feelings of guilt and a distortion of reality such that some sufferers are incapable of believing that they can repent and be helped. How can this be squared with the demand on all people to repent of their sins? Some (by no means all) mental health conditions are the result of proven physical problems within the brain itself (either present from birth or developing later – often in adolescence). How does this square with our notions of what it is to be sinful?

An example of this issue in practice is the particular challenge of addiction, one of the few mental health issues which has some explicit biblical evidence. In Galatians 5:21 Paul declares that drunkenness is a sin which will prevent those who perpetuate it from entering the Kingdom of God, and in 1 Corinthians 5:11 tells his readers not to associate with any drunkards, or even to eat with them. Such injunctions seem fairly clear cut – being a drunk is sinful. Yet we now know that addiction can cause changes in neural pathways in the brain.[6] It is not a simple matter simply to stop drinking. This does not mean that alcoholism is acceptable, or that the actions of an alcoholic should simply be deemed to be entirely beyond their control, or even that alcoholics are not culpable to some degree in their condition. It, along with a number of other mental health issues, does, however, call for a challenge to our conceptions of responsibility which will require future exploration.

redemption

There is a clash within the psychiatric profession over the extent to which particular conditions are treatable. Psychiatry has for many years divided the field of mental health between personality disorders and mental illness.[7] The latter is an absence of health, the former a "deeply ingrained maladaptive pattern of behaviour."[8] This distinction matters because some psychiatrists hold that certain personality disorders are sufficiently serious and maladaptive as to be untreatable.[9]

For Christian practitioners in this field such a conclusion raises profound theological difficulties. First, what does it mean for repentance if someone is unable to conceive of right and wrong in any meaningful sense? Second, what does it mean for a Christian vision of redemption if some people have a disorder which leads to them committing evil acts, apparently without any ability to prevent themselves from doing so?

This is a serious issue, but there are relatively few Christian initiatives in the sphere of severe personality disorders (outside of chaplaincy in prison and forensic settings). Attention to the theology around treatability and how it relates to redemption is something which could be built upon.

reconciliation

Closely tied to responsibility and redemption is a third critical theological tenet, that of reconciliation. Reconciliation is one of the seven sacraments of the Catholic Church, with the idea being that through penance and confession Christians are reconciled with God and returned to right relationship rather than one which is divided by sin. Jesus' sacrifice and death is the ultimate reconciliation of humanity as a whole with God, as 2 Corinthians 5:8-20 makes clear:

> All this is from God, who reconciled us to himself through Christ and gave us the ministry of reconciliation: that God was reconciling the world to himself in Christ, not counting people's sins against them. And he has committed to us the message of reconciliation. We are therefore Christ's ambassadors, as though God were making his appeal through us. We implore you on Christ's behalf: be reconciled to God.

That would suggest that reconciliation is primarily a matter of being individually reconciled to God. This is certainly important for many people experiencing mental health difficulties who struggle with their faith, and would like to have care paid to their spiritual needs as well as to medical treatment.

More broadly, there are several further aspects of reconciliation worth considering. The first is that one common theme to emerge from the interviews conducted for this scoping study was the importance of being able to accept a mental health problem and then learning how to live with it. One interviewee compared the experience to diabetes – "You have to learn what you have and then how the medication and treatment affect you". This, in a sense, is a sort of *internal reconciliation* which may require spiritual assistance and pastoral care on the part of the Church.

There is also the broader question of reconciliation into the community. Many mental health issues isolate people from communities. Some, like anxiety, particular phobias, or low self-esteem prevent people from integrating themselves. Others, particularly at the more clinical end of the spectrum, such as personality disorders and psychosis, may lead to sufferers being actively detained under a section of the Mental Health Act or removed from society. Others carry a stigma, which makes it hard for people to (re-)integrate into society either after or before recovery.

This is a challenge to Christians, partly because of the relational nature of human beings (see above), which demands that we help people to build the Common Good by communicating with one another. Moreover, the healing ministry of Jesus reveals the importance of re-integration of people into the community once they are healed. The healing miracles of Jesus in the gospels reveal the power of God, and they heal those afflicted with a range of (generally physical) ailments. They also, however, fit into a wider message about reconciliation. Healing leprosy (Mark 1:40-45, Luke 17:11-19) is striking because lepers were not only sick, but social pariahs barred from integration into community. The haemorrhaging woman (Mark 5:21-43 and others) was sick, but also deemed to be unclean, and therefore unable to be fully part of the community. It is notable that after healing the lepers, Jesus orders them to go and see the priest – since a priest was needed to declare someone fit to rejoin society.

How does the Church today help people with mental health issues integrate into society, either while they are suffering or after recovery? The evidence from the initial interviews was mixed. A number of schemes and programmes have been developed which are designed to reduce stigma and find ways of including a more integrated community, but there were also concerns that this was a patchy process and that there was significant scope for improvement.

Each of these three themes – responsibility, redemption and reconciliation – raises serious theological questions. Further research will be required to ascertain how churches, Christian mental health practitioners, people experiencing mental health issues and medical professionals respectively view these issues and to propose new models.

further work that is needed in the light of the theological material:

- Theological work is required around the doctrines of responsibility, redemption and reconciliation that specifically considers the issue of mental health as a challenge to traditional Christian approaches.

chapter 2 – references

1   See Emily Wood' Mental Health and The Church Community', *Chrism* Vol. 53 No.2 Autumn 2016.

2   This is summarised in *The Compendium of the Social Doctrine of the Church* (Pontifical Council for Justice and Peace, 2004, 34) as "Being a person in the image and likeness of God … involves existing in a relationship, in relation to the other, because God himself, one and triune, is the communion of the Father, of the Son and of the Holy Spirit".

3   A good summary of the idea as expressed in British Catholicism is the 1996 statement from the Catholic Bishops' Conference of England and Wales 'The Common Good and the Catholic Church's Social Teaching', http://www.catholic-ew.org.uk/Catholic-News-Media-Library/Archive-Media-Assets/Files/CBCEW-Publications/The-Common-Good-and-the-Catholic-Church-s-Social-Teaching

4   A point made repeatedly in interviews was the struggle to verbalise mental health experiences in a meaningful way to others.

5   See for example Theos research on Catholic charities and their focus on relationships – Ryan, *Catholic Charities and Catholic Social Teaching Today: Need and Opportunity* (Theos, 2016), and Theos research that emphasises the effect of relationships on wellbeing – Spencer et al, *Religion and Wellbeing: Assessing the Evidence* (Theos, 2016).

6   This is the theory of "neuroplasticity" which has been developing since the 1970s and is now well established.

7   Beer and Pocock, *Mad, Bad or Sad? A Christian approach to antisocial behaviour and mental disorder*, Christian Medical Fellowship (2006).

8   The World Health Organization (WHO), International Classification of Diseases 10

9   Beer and Pocock *Mad, Bad or Sad?* p. 90.

3

mapping Christian initiatives in the field

What counts as a Christian initiative into the realm of mental health is not clear cut. It depends, for example, on where you draw the lines of the definition of mental health. The World Health Organization says that "mental health is defined as a state of well-being in which every individual realizes his or her own potential, can cope with the normal stresses of life, can work productively and fruitfully, and is able to make a contribution to her or his community." (WHO, 2014)

That definition is fine, but not hugely helpful in delineating a clear area of focus. It could, and in a sense does, include every aspect of social interaction, identity and activity. Everything, from chemical and physical disorders and disabilities to purely social constructs can be included within such a bracket. Organisations and individuals who work in the mental health sector can incorporate a range that extends from the primarily medical (some of which are almost 'mechanical' in the sense that they are seeking to fix something that has gone physically wrong), to those whose work is more straightforwardly pastoral (perhaps providing a listening ear, or a respite service).

The spread of possible initiatives is, therefore, enormous. The grid below has attempted to distinguish between some broad categories of initiative, drawing on those used by the organisation Mind and adding in those to which our attention was drawn in interviews and discussions. The grid itself is not a systematic study, which would require a larger and more sustained project using quantitative data and a broader national survey. It is, however, indicative of the spread. What it demonstrates is that there are a great many Christian initiatives across a huge range of areas, though they are often highly localised, small scale and under the radar.

The grid also tries to draw some distinction between primary and secondary engagements. Primary engagements are those in which a project has been specifically designed to address or at least minister to a particular mental health issue. Christian Counselling, for example, has a specific and conscious task in working with the recently bereaved and challenging that issue. There are also, however, secondary engagements. For example, sticking with the issue of bereavement, it has been recognised in several studies that there is great value in ritualised closure (e.g. funerals) in helping with bereavement. Christian funerals are not primarily about helping with bereavement, but they certainly have an impact. In practice, it is even more difficult to identify these secondary engagements than primary ones.

Mental health issue	Description	Primary engagement	Secondary engagement
Anger	Anger that is unhealthy, destructive and has a broader negative impact on health	Domestic violence intervention project, Southwark	
Intervention designed to help prevent domestic violence.			
Anxiety and panic attacks	Anxiety is a general term for several disorders that cause nervousness, fear, apprehension, and worrying	Christian counselling and therapy	Prayer groups
		Mindfulness projects	
Christian counselling is used to confront a number of the issues on this list and is counselling from a distinctively Christian mind-set and background. See also the section on stress below, which could be taken as pre-emptive work against the development of anxiety and panic attacks.			
Bereavement	Support for those suffering from the loss of a loved one	Catholic Children's Society Westminster "Rainbows" bereavement work	Funerals
		Brentwood Catholic children's Society	
		SVP	Theology concerning an afterlife
		Christian Counselling and therapy	
It is difficult to define the full spread of work relating to bereavement, since the issue can arise in almost any pastoral setting. Some children's societies have developed specific programmes of work to talk to children about bereavement. At the secondary level there is a body of evidence to support the idea that ritualised closure, as offered by funerals, and a belief in the afterlife has a significant impact on people's ability to deal with bereavement.			

Mental health issue	Description	Primary engagement	Secondary engagement
Bipolar Affective Disorder	A mental health disorder that has serious effects on people's moods	Livability	Chaplaincy work in mental health trusts
Livability and other organisations have focused on making it possible for bipolar sufferers to participate fully within church and society more broadly. There is evidence that chaplaincy work can aid recovery times for those within the medical system.			
Body Dysmorphic Disorder	An anxiety disorder related to body image	Beloved scheme	Mental health chaplaincy
Beloved is one of a number of schemes designed to confront body image issues in schools. There is evidence that chaplaincy work can aid recovery times for those within the medical system.			
Carer support	Work providing respite and support to those caring for mental health needs of others	Befriending services (multiple)	
		Holiday camps	
		Christian day centre services	
		Drop in cafés	
There is a significant range of carer support services run by Christian groups. Among others these include a drop-in café for nurses, where they can relax and receive pastoral support if they want it. There are also a number of charities specialising in visiting the elderly or mentally ill and supporting carers that way, and a number running day centres for more serious issues. For many years there have been holiday camps run by Christian charities that specialise in supporting people with particular mental disabilities and illnesses.			
Demonic influences, oppression and possession	Included here despite note of caution expressed in section above.	Deliverance ministry (exorcism)	
Exorcism is a growing phenomenon in the UK. Some analysis is provided above.			

Mental health issue	Description	Primary engagement	Secondary engagement
Clergy mental health support	Includes both work with clergy suffering from mental health problems, and support for clergy dealing with mental health issues in others	Guild of Health	
		Diocesan workshops and training	
		Mental health matters	
		Mind and Soul	
		Flourish scheme	
		Health in Mind	
		St Luke's Healthcare for the Clergy	
		London School of Theology therapy and counselling training	
		Holy Rood House	
		Livability	

Some of these projects (e.g. the Flourish scheme in Northern Ireland) are designed to work with clergy who are themselves struggling with a mental health issue. Others are designed to help them work with members of their congregations who are experiencing mental health problems, usually by providing training in things like mental health first aid.

Dementia	Chronic disorder linked to memory loss, personality change and loss of reasoning skills. There is debate as to how far this should be included as a mental health issue – but it is treated as such by a number of services and organisations – hence its inclusion here	Pastoral care groups	
		Befriending services	
		Christian elderly people's homes	
		FaithActon Friendly Spaces	
		Livability Dementia Friendly Church project	
		Dementia cafés	

An area of fast growing concern, there are now quite a few services designed for supporting people with dementia. There are, for example, a growing number of cafés designed to support the pastoral needs of those with dementia and their carers. At the more all-encompassing end of services are the various elderly people's homes run by Christian organisations.

35

Mental health issue	Description	Primary engagement	Secondary engagement
Depression	A prolonged low mood, which in extreme cases can be life-threatening due to suicidal tendencies	Christian Counselling	Mental health chaplaincy
		Dealing with depression courses (Holy Trinity Brompton and others)	
		Retreat and therapy centres (e.g. Holy Rood House)	

Christian counselling, as the name suggests, is counselling that operates with a specifically Christian worldview. There are now several courses that have been developed by different churches to support people with depression, as well as several Christian retreat centres that have developed an expertise in the area.

Mental health issue	Description	Primary engagement	Secondary engagement
Development Disorders (e.g. ADHD, autism)	Includes a range of disorders that often develop in childhood and adolescence including autism spectrum disorders	Children's Societies	
		Christian counselling and therapy	
		Livability	

Several Christian children's societies work on early identification of development disorders. Other schemes revolve around helping those with development disorders to live a full life and be included in the church and society.

Mental health issue	Description	Primary engagement	Secondary engagement
Dissociative disorder	Dissociation is a symptom of several mental health problems and can include such issues as amnesia and identity confusion, among others	Christian counselling and therapy	Mental health chaplaincy

As with several disorders that are more clinical in how they tend to be treated there are fewer direct Christian initiatives on this issue.

Mental health issue	Description	Primary engagement	Secondary engagement
Drug and alcohol abuse	Addictions and substance abuse. Projects here also include treatment, prevention and support for family members	Alcoholics anonymous	Evidence of Pentecostalism and reduced alcoholism in developing world[1]
		Calix service	
		Betel, Remar, Yeldall Manor and other drug and addiction charities	
		Addiction support programmes	
		CAP Release scheme	
		Intervention groups	

A range of schemes are currently underway, including various addiction support and intervention groups at a local level, of which AA is the best known. There are also several charities providing rehabilitation facilities. An interesting secondary intervention has been indicated by the work done analysing the effect of converting to Pentecostal Christianity and resulting reductions in alcoholism in parts of the developing world.

Eating problems	These include anorexia and bulimia	Mind and Soul training	
		Therapy work – including Catholic Children's Society Westminster	
		Christian counselling and therapy	

Mind and Soul provide training to churches and Christian groups in how to respond to eating problems. Counselling works with the sufferers themselves. See also work on self-esteem below, which is often closely connected.

Hearing voices	There are several reasons for hearing voices, which can include extreme cases of people hearing commands in their heads that cause them to act against their own best interest	Royal College of Psychiatrists, special interest group in spirituality	
		Deliverance ministry/exorcism	

For Christians there is a difficulty here, which is the inclination to take the idea of divine commands seriously. The Royal College of Psychiatrists' spirituality interest group work is to identify routes forward on that issue. In the case of suspected demonic possessions, exorcists remain in demand.

Mental health issue	Description	Primary engagement	Secondary engagement
Hypomania and mania	Overactive and excitable behaviour	Christian counselling and therapy	Mental health chaplaincy
As with several disorders that are more clinical in how they tend to be treated there are fewer direct Christian initiatives on this issue.			
Loneliness	The subject of significant public attention at present. Among those particularly at risk are the elderly, migrants isolated by a lack of English, and, increasingly, the younger generation	Befriending services (many)	Church services
		Faith Action Friendly Spaces	Bingo groups
		C.f CUF mapping work	
Loneliness has been the subject of a large number of recent studies, notably by the Church Urban Fund.[2] There are a vast number of projects in this space, including many befriending services which specialise in visiting the elderly or lonely (see for example the work of the St Vincent de Paul Society).			
Mental health first aid	Training in immediate responses to mental health issues	Livability	
		Flourish	
		Mind and Soul	
		Welcome Me as I Am	
Training in this area is now provided by a number of schemes, which train up clergy and volunteers across a number of churches to recognise and respond to mental health issues.			
Obsessive Compulsive Disorder (OCD)	Obsessive and unwanted thoughts, and resulting drive to compulsively perform particular actions	Christian counselling and therapy	Mental health chaplaincy work
As with several disorders that are more clinical in how they tend to be treated there are fewer direct Christian initiatives on this issue.			
Paranoia	Can include delusions of persecution, jealousy and exaggerated sense of own importance	Christian counselling and therapy	Mental health chaplaincy work
As with several disorders that are more clinical in how they tend to be treated there are fewer direct Christian initiatives on this issue.			

Mental health issue	Description	Primary engagement	Secondary engagement
Personality disorders	A range of disorders, some of which are quite rare, but which can have severe consequences in terms of maladaptive behaviours	Christian counselling and therapy	Mental health chaplaincy work
As with several disorders that are more clinical in how they tend to be treated there are fewer direct Christian initiatives on this issue.			
Phobia	Covers a set of irrational fears including agoraphobia (fear of the outdoors)	Christian counselling and therapy	Mental health chaplaincy work
As with several disorders that are more clinical in how they tend to be treated there are fewer direct Christian initiatives on this issue.			
Postnatal depression	Depression following childbirth	Mums' chaplaincy	Mums and tots support groups
		Parenting classes and support	
		Parent mentoring	
The mums' chaplaincy programme helps support new mothers. Parent mentoring is a scheme run by several Christian groups to help support new parents.			
Post-Traumatic Stress Disorder (PTSD)	An anxiety disorder promoted by past traumatic experiences	Christian recovery centres	Chaplaincy
		Christian counselling and therapy	Armed Forces Christian Fellowship
Christian recovery centres help people recovering from PTSD. In a secondary sense, chaplaincy and the Armed Forces Fellowship help support members of the military (and in the case of chaplaincy, emergency services and healthcare professions too) with their pastoral and spiritual needs, including support with PTSD.			
Psychosis	A perception of reality at odds with how others perceive it	Awareness raising schemes	Mental health chaplaincy work
		Christian counselling and therapy	
There are a number of efforts at informing people about the reality of mental illness. Psychosis is one of the more oft-misunderstood terms in the field and several schemes deal with it at some length.			

Mental health issue	Description	Primary engagement	Secondary engagement
Schizoaffective disorder	A condition in which there is a combination of schizophrenic symptoms and mood disorders		Mental health chaplaincy work
As with several disorders that are more clinical in how they tend to be treated there are fewer direct Christian initiatives on this issue.			
Schizophrenia	Chronic condition affecting how a person thinks, feels and behaves. Can include an apparent losing touch with reality		Mental health chaplaincy work
As with several disorders that are more clinical in how they tend to be treated there are fewer direct Christian initiatives on this issue.			
Seasonal affective disorder (SAD)	Depression associated with seasonal change (especially during winter)		Mental health chaplaincy work
As with several disorders that are more clinical in how they tend to be treated there are fewer direct Christian initiatives on this issue.			
Self-esteem	Sense of self-worth. Low self-esteem is linked closely to a number of mental health issues, including drug and alcohol abuse, eating problems and depression	Beloved scheme for teenage girls	
		Schemes designed to empower those with mental illness within a church setting	
		Kids Matter work with parents	
		Chaplaincy programmes on self-esteem	
Building self-esteem has become a stated aim of chaplaincies in a number of settings including schools (particularly with teenage girls) and prisons. Other schemes focus on empowering individuals to build self-esteem by getting them safely involved in church and community life with a support network to help them.			

Mental health issue	Description	Primary engagement	Secondary engagement
Self-harm	Self-abuse as a result of mental illness	Children's Societies	
		Residential rehabilitation	
		Christian counselling and therapy	
		Youthscape	

Since self-harm is generally a symptom of mental illness, rather than a mental health issue itself, this should be read in conjunction with other mental health issues. However, particularly among Christian charities with a focus on children and teenagers there are programmes designed to directly address the issue of self-harm.

Mental health issue	Description	Primary engagement	Secondary engagement
Sleep problems	Insomnia and related sleep issues are often linked to other mental health issues	Christian counselling and therapy	

As with several disorders that are more clinical in how they tend to be treated (in this case often with use of sleeping drugs) there are fewer direct Christian initiatives on this issue.

Mental health issue	Description	Primary engagement	Secondary engagement
Stress	Pressure and emotional strain. When severe it is closely linked to a range of other mental and physical health issues	Young Catholics stress project	Meditation and prayer groups
		Mindfulness in schools project – Norwich	
		Children's Societies	
		Mindfulness projects	
		Workplace chaplaincy programmes	
		University chaplaincy student support schemes	

There are projects that confront stress in many different contexts, from workplace-based chaplaincy and mindfulness projects, to university schemes (including Brunel University chaplaincy's "rabbit café" which brings in rabbits for students to play with) and projects that are particularly targeted at children and teenagers. As a secondary engagement there is a wealth of evidence to suggest that meditation and prayer can help reduce levels of stress and anxiety.[3]

Mental health issue	Description	Primary engagement	Secondary engagement
Suicidal feelings	Considering the possibility of suicide	Flourish scheme	
		Beachy Head chaplaincy	
		Christian counselling and therapy	
		Anthem of Hope	
		Residential care	
Since suicide is often a response to a severe mental health issue this section should not be read in isolation from various others on this list, including depression. There are several Christian charities working specifically on suicide intervention – including the flourish scheme run by the Lighthouse suicide prevention charity in Northern Ireland and the Anthem of Hope charity. The Beachy Head chaplaincy is perhaps the most direct form of suicide prevention since their role is to walk the cliffs at Beachy head, Britain's most popular suicide destination.			
Supporting others with suicidal feelings	Work supporting others who have considered or attempted suicide	Flourish scheme	
		Anthem of Hope	
		Mental health first aid schemes	
		London School of Theology therapy and counselling training	
Clearly there is a fair amount of overlap with suicide prevention work, and in some cases bereavement work, as above. Otherwise there are several projects working in first aid and helping people (often clergy) to counsel and be alongside suicide.			
Supported living	Housing and support for those living with severe mental health needs	Father Hudson's Care	
		Catholic Care, Leeds	
There are several charities and organisations, including Catholic Care and Father Hudson's Care, who provide supported living services, including assisted living residential care.			

Mental health issue	Description	Primary engagement	Secondary engagement
Resources and awareness raising	Variety of schemes to de-stigmatise mental health and raise awareness	Mind and Soul	
		Keeping Faith in Mind	
		Christian Medical Fellowship Resources	
		Welcome Me As I Am	
		Guild of Health and St Raphael	
		Livability	
		London School of Theology therapy and counselling training	
		Mental Health Matters	
		Ethnic minority mental health resources	
		Faith Action: Friendly Places	
		Catholic Mental Health Project	
There are now quite a few organisations that have specialised in raising awareness of these issues and producing resources to help churches, organisations and individuals respond to mental health issues.			
Other		Music for Older People with Mental Health Problems	
		Kids Matter work with parent support groups	
		'Emotional Wellbeing Project' with People who are Homeless	
		Travellers in prison project/ Irish chaplaincy	
These three projects work across a range of mental health issues but within quite specific settings.			

future work needed in light of the empirical evidence:

- The table above is an indicative look at the work that is currently going on. It is not by any means exhaustive of the whole spectrum and future work will be needed to map with more clarity the full scope of Christian activity, e.g. where it is going, how extensive is it, who it is run by, what groups are involved, who it is serving, the nature of the existing relationships between the project and relevant medical and/ or statutory authorities, how well funded and resourced it is, how professionally run it is, etc..

chapter 3 – references

1   See Harold Koenig, *The Healing Power of Faith: How Belief and Prayer Can Help You Triumph Over Disease* (New York, NY: Touchstone, 2001).

2   See 'A Silent Epidemic: How can we share one another's loneliness?', Church Urban Fund (2015) and 'Connecting Communities: The impact of loneliness and opportunities for churches to respond', Church Urban Fund (2016).

3   See Spencer et al *Religion and Wellbeing: Assessing the Evidence*, Theos (2016) pp. 34-37, 72-77.

Christian work in mental health: how effective is it?

Christian projects: helpful or unhelpful?

There is mixed evidence on the helpfulness of Christian projects in the mental health sphere. There is a mounting body of evidence that suggests that religious belief aids resilience in responding to traumatic events and leads to faster recovery from mental health problems. More broadly there is a positive correlation between religion and wellbeing, particularly for those involved in social participation (e.g. religious services). A number of studies, across a range of contexts, have borne out those conclusions.

If that provides some evidence for the helpfulness of religion in general for personal wellbeing and mental health, there is also some reason for seeing the public usefulness of Christian projects. The number of initiatives at a local level is significant and such interventions often serve as productive partners with secular and statutory bodies. Effective Christian initiatives can reduce the burden on the NHS or social services, serving a public good. In fact a recent report from the Local Government Association in partnership with FaithAction made precisely that point.

However, it would be a mistake to claim that the situation is simply positive. At the personal level, there is evidence that faith can have negative consequences for mental health and wellbeing. For example, those suffering with obsessive and/or compulsive behaviours or anxiety can find religion reinforces negative behaviour. In some cases this is due to an accentuation of feelings of guilt, or encourages obsessive behaviour under the guise of rituals.

A recent report from the Oasis Foundation also drew attention to the impact on the wellbeing of LGB (lesbian, gay and bisexual) individuals where churches failed to recognise or accept their sexuality. Though some of those findings have been contested, there does seem to be reason for concern in this regard.

There is also a concern over the mental health of clergy. This has been identified as something approaching a crisis in more than one denomination. There is an increasing interest in meeting that need, but the broader question must revolve around what it is in the Christian model of ministry that is leading so many clergy to be so vulnerable in the first place?

Nor is the public good of Christian initiatives a simply positive story. Aside from broader concerns about the role of faith based organisations operating in the public square and the 'dangers' of proselytism,[1] there was also a reported frustration with mental health interventions in particular. The mental health researcher Emily Wood, for example, recounts the frustration of many mental health professionals with patients who have gone off their medication because of advice they have received at church and promptly relapsed, setting their recovery back. In the scoping study we attempted to explore some of these issues in interviews. Making a case for how to ensure that initiatives are maximally beneficial would be a proposed outcome for future research.

the work of Christian groups, in their eyes

In order to get an initial understanding of the nature, success and challenges of Christian activity in addressing problems of mental health, we conducted 15 in-depth interviews with people who were working in various roles within mental health. These included people with an overview of a project within a denomination or region, direct care providers and chaplains, representatives of charities delivering training and projects and people with experience of suffering mental health problems within a Church setting. These interviews were designed to be indicative rather than comprehensive. In order to strengthen, deepen and add fine detail to sustain the tentative conclusions arrived at below, we recognise the need for a far more extensive study taking in a broader range of interviews. The contours of that potential research are outlined alongside the findings. That caveat noted, there are a number of research questions which emerged from the interviews below.

what's worked well?

Several interviewees identified the value of creating resources, such as the Mental Health Access Pack, which help to educate Christian groups on the sorts of mental health issues that exist and how to respond. One of the persistent challenges when it comes to mental health is the lack of public awareness and knowledge of particular conditions and how to respond to those suffering without making mistakes or being seen as insensitive.

One interviewee, who provided training in mental health services to local churches, reported a constant worry from people that "they were saying the wrong thing" and as a result didn't want to get involved in the same way they did with other services like food banks. Another, who had suffered with mental health issues themself described people "clamming up and not making eye contact" rather than talking normally about it. They also described the sense of shock from people who could not believe that they were suffering from depression – they didn't understand how it manifested itself.

Good resources, including videos, reports, and short guides, which helped to explain mental health to people and how they could help, had all received very positive feedback. Keeping these resources up to date, accessible and online was, however, proving a challenge for those (the majority) who lacked significant institutional backing. One, for example, who manages a website with resources and links had struggled to keep it going due to other commitments and health issues and had found it very difficult to find someone else to take it on or to commit any funding to supporting it, despite a consistently high level of use and positive feedback.

Conferences and events designed to help people understand and respond to mental health issues were also reported as having been successful – though there was a challenge there in having the people available to provide such events. The lack of available funding for many organisations left them reliant on getting expenses paid by those to whom they were speaking, which was having a detrimental effect on their impact. There was also simply a limited pool of people with sufficient expertise to provide training. One or two interviewees recorded concerns about the quality of information at some events. One, reflecting on an experience of an event at a Christian festival which had a small session on mental health, said they had been concerned about some of the information being provided which was "clearly not helpful, or worse even harmful".

Some of the most effective work was done with young people. The vast majority of mental health sufferers develop symptoms in childhood or adolescence which in many cases can be significantly helped by early intervention. Several Christian groups were working in schools and with young people and had developed intentional means of identifying possible mental health problems at an early stage, as well as training other staff to do the same. One interviewee described as a dream future scenario a situation in which they'd be able to "train every teacher and member in staff in identification of mental health issues at an early stage". It is difficult to provide hard assessments of the long term benefits of such a strategy, but given the numbers of children that some of these charities reached it seems likely that the potential benefits are significant.

In line with the note above on mental health among the clergy, an increasing number of schemes and strategies are designed with a more specifically clerical focus. Many of these revolve around self-care, and perhaps the most interesting is the Flourish scheme part-funded by the public health authorities of Northern Ireland to train clergy in self-care. This had been brought in due to the recognition that clergy are disproportionately vulnerable, and also see a disproportionate number of people suffering with mental health issues. Nor are the people that they see necessarily at the early or minor stages of sickness, but many reported encountering people seeking help suffering with severe psychosis, schizophrenia and other significant clinical issues. One interviewee described the nature of the work done by clergy as "the thick end of the wedge" when it came to encountering people seeking help with mental health issues. Programmes designed to meet the needs of clergy had, accordingly, often been deemed to be particularly helpful.

Finally, several interviewees spoke of the success of projects designed for the pastoral care of carers – such as drop in cafés. One interviewee had had some success in bringing together several of these into an informal group to discuss best practice and experiences. They had found that several had been quite successful in finding partners with NHS and local government and had received excellent feedback from service users.

what's proved difficult?

It will probably come as little surprise to anyone working within the faith-based charity sector that funding was a serious issue. Interestingly, however, the reasons given for struggling to find funding were quite varied. Some had had issues getting statutory money or partnerships with secular bodies (whether the NHS, local government or education bodies).

For some this was due, or often it felt as if it were due simply to being a faith based organisations. One, for example, applied for tendered projects with local government contracts, but had faced criticism and opposition in the local press and from particular pressure groups which they believed had had an impact on their ability to win contracts. In that case senior staff members had actually been criticised by name in the press by local secular and humanist groups on the basis that they were "bigoted" and would be "unable to deal with issues of homosexuality and bullying as a faith body". This was despite the fact that as part of the bid the charity in question had already agreed to abide by any rules the school might have had in place on those issues.

For others the challenge had been not so much with statutory bodies as with churches. While most reported high levels of support from church leadership and local churches, few had been backed with significant (or often sufficient) funding for their work. The issue went beyond money. Several felt there was little sense in which they were part of an overall strategy. The issue was taken seriously at national level, but there was a perception that this did not translate into much by way of a cohesive response. There appeared to be some duplication of roles, and some parts of the country which were far better served than others. Some had had to work hard to establish their projects and felt abandoned by the church, which had said it was supportive but seemed unable to provide either financial or even networking resources in any sort of way. One interviewee had "just given up" trying to get information out of various dioceses on what they were doing in the field, because they seemed unable to ever update anyone or provide information in advance.

More broadly, while there was a real desire to engage with the issue of mental health at both a local and national level, and many interviewees reported warm meetings with leadership and being oversubscribed for events and training at local and regional levels, there was nonetheless a sense that as a whole the church did not know how it wanted to respond. One organisation that provided events and training had become frustrated that too little happened as a result of their efforts. They had come to think that many local churches booked speakers or training simply as a means of "ticking a box" or because it seemed like an interesting thing to do that week, but had no intention of developing anything on the back of it. The organisation had adapted to that by refusing requests that were not part of a wider scheme or project with some bigger aim on the issue.

how do they know if they've had an impact?

The ability to calculate the impact of charity work is a huge issue that extends far beyond the mental health sector. It is a notoriously difficult question which, to be answered with any sort of scientific rigour, requires an extensive data set (which is often impossible for small scale operations). Much depends on the sort of impact being measured (for example, how does one evaluate the social aspect of a particular project, or the spiritual impact?) and the particular mental health issue being addressed (some conditions being easier to address than others). In practice, proposing a model of impact assessment that is equally applicable across the many forms of mental health issue presented in chapter 1, and across the different sizes and types of Christian initiatives outlined in chapter 3 is always going to be difficult, and probably near impossible.

In addition to this, there was also a frustration with a lot of the impact discourse (models of how to record impact and effectiveness that range from simple recording of activity to complex analysis of outcomes) expressed across several interviews.

For example, one respondent working in an education context described how a growing number of schools and agencies demanded an increasingly broad range of evidence, including star ratings, certificates and others. While they were always keen to make sure that they provided whatever the schools wanted, the interviewee believed that most of the measures were essentially subjective measures dressed up to look like scientific evidence. The interviewee believed, in common with several others, that a lot of the work they were doing (which in this case tended to focus at the less severe end of the mental health issue spectrum) was better assessed simply by looking at whether there had been a difference in the behaviour and happiness of the clients with whom they were working.

Another interviewee had grown frustrated by the Church's obsession with numerical evidence of growth and impact at the expense of more obviously Christian approaches to success. A number of interviewees had moved to quite a qualitative-heavy means of measuring their work, often gathering stories or collecting qualitative evidence that looked at "the journey" on which their service users had been on.

Of course, there needs to be caution in this. Having a robust critical attitude that seeks to constantly improve performance is generally healthy and guards against complacency and bad practice. Those charities, churches and groups that work closely with publicly funded bodies cannot escape the need to provide evidence in line with the practices expected of those organisations. A sense of balance needs to be found between the need to provide quantitative evidence of the sort that is required in many public settings on the one hand, and authentic Christian conceptions of value on the other.

There is already, in fact, a number of different data- and quantitative-evidence-based models that have achieved some success in different settings. Some of these primarily measure activity (keeping track of the number of clients seen, under what circumstances and with what measurable outputs). These are important, if obviously limited in terms of assessing qualitatively what difference such initiatives have made.

Others are more sophisticated. Chaplaincy in various settings is developing more robust impact models that might begin to demonstrate the particular difference such a service might make. Developing this has been an explicit concern and recommendation of the Scottish government to NHS trusts in Scotland.[2] This has led, among other things, to experimentation with the American PROMIS (Patient Recorded Outcome Measurement Information System) which provides a number of assessment tools by which to measure the wellbeing and impact of different interventions on patients. Pilot projects like these are being experimented within an increasing range of NHS chaplaincy contexts both in Scotland and elsewhere across the UK.

An interesting example of this in practice is the research conducted by Peter Kevern and others looking at chaplaincy in primary care settings and their impact on wellbeing.[3] This research, which analysed data from patients before and after using the chaplaincy service, using the Warwick and Edinburgh Mental Wellbeing Scale (WEMWBS) demonstrated (albeit with a limited sample in a particular location) a notable positive impact on wellbeing from using the service.

Methods like that require a good data set, which is often difficult for smaller services, but do demonstrate some of the possibilities which may lie in the future for chaplaincy and other Christian initiatives in the mental health sector.

how do Christian bodies in the field view their relationship with secular bodies?

Testimony from our interviewees was very mixed on this issue. As reported above, some felt they had had difficulties in securing funding or partnerships due to their status as faith-based organisations. This seemed to be an issue which varied hugely depending on geographical location (different councils seemed to take radically different standpoints on how willing they were to work with faith organisations) and to some extent depending on the sort of work in question.

Organisations working with children or vulnerable adults, unsurprisingly, had to demonstrate very high levels of safeguarding procedure and often felt they had to work hard to justify their rights to hold a faith standpoint.

This had not stopped a huge amount of work, including chaplaincy, schools work, youth clubs, and prison programmes with a significant mental health element from functioning in a range of settings. It did, however, force many organisations working in those settings to do a lot of bureaucratic work, and some felt that the hoops they were forced to jump through by virtue of being a faith body were significantly more extensive than those of other organisations, regardless of the ethos that might have underpinned their work.[4] One mental health chaplain, for example, recorded that they constantly felt the need to justify their own existence to the "Deloittes-style managers" that the NHS had brought in. They felt particularly targeted, with more and more requirements than anyone else they knew within the trust.

Balancing this picture, however, were other interviewees who reported extremely positive reactions from secular bodies. One interviewee, who ran training in mental health first aid for churches, reported great support from the local NHS trust, which had helped with resources and in training volunteers. Others had developed close relationships in delivering services to help carers, nurses and others dealing with mental health issues from a pastoral point of view. There were similar positive stories relating to local government funding for particular programmes. The most striking example, however, was the Flourish scheme in Northern Ireland which was delivered by a secular suicide prevention charity and funded by the public health authority. The rationale for this had been that there was a serious need to address the mental health of clergy, who serve a key role in confronting mental health issues in others and are often important local community figures. The work was officially recognised in the Chief Medical Officer of Northern Ireland's 2014 report.[5]

how good, from the perspective of Christian organisations, is the medical profession at dealing with spiritual and religious issues?

The place of religion and spirituality in the medical profession (particularly as concerns mental health) has changed significantly in recent years. Until quite recently, the perception was that the medical and psychiatric professions were quite hostile to questions of faith and spirituality. In fact, a number of studies pointed to a "spirituality gap" which suggested that those patients in the medical system with mental health issues were disproportionately religious, and wanted spirituality taken seriously, but those working in the medical profession were disproportionately atheist and hostile to the idea of faith.[6]

According to several of our interviewees, a great deal of progress has been made in that regard. One big development has come from the work of the Spirituality and Psychiatry Special Interest Group at the Royal College of Psychiatrists. This group, which was set up in order to provide psychiatrists with a space in which to reflect on the place of religion and spirituality in psychiatry has been very successful at producing resources and gaining a following in the profession. The NHS in both England and Scotland now advises a greater place for questions of spirituality than was previously the case.

Nonetheless, there are still some issues here. One is a difficulty in taking *religion*, as opposed to simply *spirituality*, seriously. Religion is seen, according to some interviewees, as something which can be outsourced to local religious figures, regardless of their expertise on mental health issues, while spirituality is something which is done by professionals. There is also a perception that spirituality is dealt with as a pastoral issue, rather than something that has a meaningful medical impact.

Other interviewees noted that although progress has been made in taking spirituality seriously at an institutional level, there was still a great deal of fear about what was or wasn't appropriate. Prominent media stories about medical professionals being sacked or disciplined for praying with patients or manifesting their own beliefs had apparently caused some to try and avoid religious questions altogether for fear of being accused of having been inappropriate. This was recorded as an issue by mental health chaplains, who reported the fears of nurses and fellow colleagues who were no longer sure of their ground. Clarity on those issues was something which several interviewees felt would be beneficial within the medical profession.

future work in light of the above

- Though we have interviewed a number of Christians on their experiences within secular settings, there is clearly another side to the story and we need more research assessing what secular and medical bodies think about, and how they respond to, Christian initiatives, in particular exploring where there are problems and how relations could be usefully improved.

- The challenge of impact and measurement is going to remain important. There is a pressing need for more work into designing measurable impact assessment tools for Christian (and other) projects. This would be beneficial to many, particularly smaller projects.

- We need greater networking and cohesion between Christians in order to prevent overlaps and to develop a strategy that could be more effective in some areas than the piecemeal efforts that presently exist.

- Greater clarification of the rules regarding acceptable expressions of faith in an NHS context will help staff be more confident in dealing with faith issues.

- We need further work on making the positive case for spirituality and more specifically religion in helping with mental health. There is a growing evidence base that religion (and spirituality more broadly) can be beneficial for recovery and wellbeing and that people want their spiritual and religious needs addressed within the medical and care sectors, but there is still a sense in which secular bodies have been wary about embracing such opportunities.

chapter 4 – references

1   See Bickley, *The Problem of Proselytism*, Theos (2015).

2   http://www.gov.scot/Publications/2009/01/30110659/2

3   Kevern P and Ladbury I, 'The resource implications of the Sandwell "Chaplains for Wellbeing" service: a data analysis', New Writing in Health and Social Care (2015) 2(1) pp. 47-54; McSherry W, Boughey A, and Kevern P '"Chaplains for Wellbeing" in primary care: A qualitative investigation of their perceived impact for patients' health and wellbeing', Journal of Healthcare Chaplaincy (2016), and Kevern P and Hill L, '"Chaplains for Wellbeing" in Primary Care: results of a retrospective study', Primary Healthcare Research and Development (2014), 16 (1) pp. 87-99.

4   This fining is familiar from other work on faith based organisations, including Bickley, *The Problem of Proselytism*, Theos (2015).

5   https://www.health-ni.gov.uk/sites/default/files/publications/dhssps/cmo-annual-report-2014.pdf

6   Moreira-Almeida, Koenig and Lucchett,i 'Clinical implications of spirituality to mental health: review of evidence and practical guidelines' *Revista Brasileira de Psiquiatria* (April 2014) 36(2): pp. 176-82 and Webb, 'Bridging the spirituality gap', *Australian E-Journal For The Advancement Of Mental Health* Vol. 4 , Iss. 1, (2005).

conclusions

This report has not, by any means, been intended as the last word on this issue. On the contrary, it has been a scoping study undertaken with the explicit purpose of identifying necessary future research. To that end it is possible, based on what has been undertaken here, to identify two separate areas for future work. The first set of these is theological, based on the biblical and theological evidence above. The second set is empirical, and revolves around both the task of mapping initiatives (as started with the grid above) and the evidence of the success of those initiatives.

theological

When it comes to mental health there is now an evidence base from which to claim that Christianity makes a positive difference. The Theos report *Religion and Wellbeing: Assessing the Evidence* lays out in some detail how that relationship works.[1] It demonstrates a particularly strong correlation between good mental health and participation in group religious activities (e.g. attending church), and between good mental health and high levels of subjective religiosity (i.e. if you not only religious but take those beliefs seriously). In short, the relationship between religion and mental health on the whole shows that "the more serious, genuinely held and practically-evidenced a religious commitment is, then the greater the positive impact it is likely to have on well-being".[2]

Critically, however, that tells us nothing about the content of Christianity itself. Given the potential importance of the relationship it is crucial that Christians take that issue seriously and reflect theologically on how the Church responds to mental health, so that as these questions continue to gain prominence there is already a theological apparatus in place to guide initiatives. There is a need to ensure that future responses are maximally beneficial and avoid any potential pitfalls that can come from failing to fully take into account the complexities surrounding mental health. As such there are at least three future challenges, as also laid out above:

- A re-appraisal of how we use the Bible on this topic. Rather than focusing on limited accounts of explicit mental illness, or demonic possession, more attention ought to be paid to the ability to begin building an authentic Christian language of mental health from the perspective of sufferers. Where many Christian resources currently focus on raising awareness of different mental health issues there is more to be done in terms of letting sufferers find a legitimately biblical and theological language to verbalise their own experiences.

- There is need for an analysis of the burgeoning exorcism scene in the UK in the light of concerns over how it is being used and its possible negative consequences.

- There is need for biblical resources that allow for Christians to embrace medical science and prevent the danger of "over-spiritualising" problems. There is some evidence of projects working in this space already.

empirical

Aside from theological work, we need to do more work on ensuring that Christian initiatives are maximally useful and effective. There is clearly a lot of work to be done in a field this size, and there are clearly limits in terms of finances and human resources as to how much any given church or charity can be expected to do. There is, accordingly, much to be said for finding ways to connect networks and share best practice, and to help Christian initiatives to maximize the resources that they have to be as effective as possible. Accordingly, drawing on the chapters above there are several pieces of work we can propose for the future:

- Over and above the grid of Christian initiatives provided above, we need to map with more clarity the full scope of Christian activity. Knowing the full picture will be essential before strong proposals for the future can be outlined.

- Though we have interviewed a number of Christians on their experiences within secular settings, there is clearly another side to the story and future research will be needed to assess how secular and medical bodies engage with Christian initiatives and where they feel relations could be usefully improved.

- The challenge of impact and measurement is going to remain important. Future work on designing measurable impact assessment tools for Christian projects would be beneficial to many, particularly smaller projects.

- Greater networking and cohesion between Christians would be helpful in preventing overlaps and developing a strategy which could be more effective in some areas than the piecemeal efforts that presently exist.

- Greater clarification of the rules regarding acceptable expressions of faith in an NHS context would help staff be more confident in dealing with faith issues.

- There is work to do in making the positive case for spirituality and more specifically religion in helping with mental health. There is a growing evidence base that religion (and spirituality more broadly) can be beneficial for recovery and wellbeing and that people want their spiritual and religious needs addressed within the medical and care sectors, but there is still a sense in which secular bodies have been wary about embracing such opportunities.

conclusions – references

1   Spencer et al, *Religion and Wellbeing: Assessing the Evidence*, Theos (2016).

2   Ibid. p. 6.

interviewee details

Beatrice Brandon	Archbishops' Adviser for the Healing Ministry, in the Church of England
Martyn Goss	Director, Church and Society, Exeter Diocese
Alison Hogger	Keeping Faith in Mind
Rosemary Keenan	Catholic Children's Society Westminster
Eva MacIntyre	Mental Health Matters
Brendan McCarthy	National Advisor for Medical Ethics, Mission and Public Affairs team, Church of England
Mark Meynell	Chaplain to HM Treasury and Revenue and Customs
Corin Pilling	Deputy Director, Livability
Sharon Quinn	Office Manager, Lighthouse suicide prevention charity
Gail Sainsbury	Mental Health project officer, Catholic Bishops Conference England and Wales
Gillian Straine	Director, Guild of Health and St Raphael
Rob Waller	Director, Mind and Soul Foundation and Consultant Psychiatrist
Stephen Webb	Director, Brentwood Catholic Children's Society
A group of mental health chaplains	
Anonymous	NHS psychiatrist

Previous **Theos** reports include:

Christianity and Mental Health: Theology, Activities, Potential

Ben Ryan

The issue of mental health has been gaining public attention in recent years. Awareness-raising efforts across a number of fields have significantly increased public interest and concern. There have been warnings for some time, with dire statistics from various agencies – including the astonishing claim that one in four British adults had been diagnosed with a mental health issue during their lifetime.

This report seeks to explore the question, what can (and what should) Christians do in this field? It is an effort to map the landscape as it currently exists, and to raise questions for future research.

It is our hope that this report marks the start rather than an end of a programme of work looking at Christianity and mental health issues today. The subject is important, and growing in recognition; it speaks to a number of core Christian concerns pertaining to human wholeness and peace, and there are a growing number of Christian/ church-based initiatives across the country. We hope that this and subsequent work will make a contribution towards clarifying, equipping, guiding, and inspiring serious Christian engagement with mental health problems in the UK today.

ISBN: 978-0-995

Theos